# CHRIST IN THE SEASONS OF MINISTRY

Other Books by John Killinger

*The Cup and the Waterfall*
*Prayer: The Act of Being with God*
*A Devotional Guide to John: The Gospel of Life Eternal*
*A Devotional Guide to Luke: The Gospel of Contagious Joy*
*A Sense of His Presence. The Devotional Commentary: Matthew*
*His Power in You. The Devotional Commentary: Mark*
*Bread for the Wilderness, Wine for the Journey: The Miracle of Prayer and Meditation*
*All You Lonely People, All You Lovely People*
*For God's Sake, Be Human*
*The Centrality of Preaching in the Total Task of the Ministry*
*Hemingway and the Dead Gods*
*The Failure of Theology in Modern Literature*
*World in Collapse: The Vision of Absurd Drama*
*Leave It to the Spirit: Freedom and Commitment in the New Liturgy*
*The Salvation Tree*
*The Fragile Presence: Transcendence in Modern Literature*
*Experimental Preaching*
*The Second Coming of the Church*
*The 11:00 O'Clock News and Other Experimental Sermons*
*The Loneliness of Children*
*The Thickness of Glory*

*The Word Not Bound: A One-Act Play*

# CHRIST IN THE SEASONS OF MINISTRY JOHN KILLINGER

WORD BOOKS
PUBLISHER
WACO, TEXAS

A DIVISION OF
WORD, INCORPORATED

Library of Congress Cataloging in Publication Data:
    Killinger, John.
        Christ in the seasons of ministry.

        1. Clergy—Religious life—Addresses, essays,
    lectures. 2. Clergy—Office—Addresses, essays,
    lectures. I. Title.
    BV4011.6.K54  1983    248.4'851092    83-16941

*Printed in the United States of America*

First Printing, November 1983
Second Printing, April 1984

*For*
*TERRY H. BIDDLE, JR.*
*A Friend for All Seasons*

# Contents

# Preface

The "messages" that make up this little book
were prepared in the summer of 1982 for the
ministers and students of the Princeton Institute
of Theology, where it was my privilege to be
the preacher on four successive evenings. I am
grateful to President James I. McCord, Dean
Conrad Massa, and Directors of Continuing
Education Jack Cooper and Ronald White for
their kind invitation to participate in the
Institute, and for the hospitality they and the
Institute extended to me while I was there.

## PREFACE

There are few places in the world as lovely as
Princeton in the summer, and the warmth and
cordiality of the ministers, spouses, and students
made the occasion a particularly meaningful one
for me.

As I told the audience at the Institute, I was
tempted, in the busyness of my life as a parish
minister, to follow the line of least resistance
and preach for them some "sugar sticks"—
sermons I had prepared for my congregation
and found to be particularly preachable and
capable of eliciting warm response. But I knew
my conscience would nag at me about that, and
therefore I conceived the notion of this series
on the "seasons" of ministry, which I hoped
would be useful to those present as stimulus for
rethinking their journeys in the ministerial
vocation. The response was so generous that
now I dare to offer them in print for a larger
audience.

The series is not intended to be exhaustive.
There are many things I might have said had
I been preparing lectures for the classroom
instead of sermons for the pulpit. Some of the
young preachers present, for example, felt that
I had stepped rather heavily on their toes
without giving credit for the contribution made

to the church by their idealism and determination to effect changes in the status quo. They were right, of course, and in a lecture I would have attempted a more balanced presentation. But the sermons were meant to be suggestive, not exhaustive—provocative, not definitive.

I hope the reader will find them so, and will use them as springboards to further thought and reflection on his or her own pilgrimage. Whatever the world may think of the ministry, it is still the highest calling in the world, and we spend the remainder of our lives, once we have been caught up by it, trying to comprehend and justify our presence in it.

JOHN KILLINGER

# Introduction

Christ and the seasons of ministry.
There are seasons, aren't there?
"To everything, a season . . ."
There was even a season for discovering the seasons of adult life, when the work of such persons as Erik Erikson, Charlotte Buhler, Robert White, Roger Gould, George Vaillant, Daniel Levinson, and others was going on. And there was a season for publicizing that work— a season that began with Gail Sheehy's runaway bestseller, *Passages: The Predictable Crises of Adult Life.*

And now we are in a season for appropriating the insights of all that work, for rethinking our individual lives in terms of the normative crises and solutions, for learning that on the highway of life there are certain bumps and curves which we may as well expect, so that we know when to decelerate and accelerate, when to shift our weight or our emphases, and when to enjoy the view until the next danger heaves into sight.

The problem is, of course, that danger follows danger in such rapid and continuous sequence that we are never really out of it, but must learn to find the enjoyment of life in the midst of our problems, while we are trying to navigate. There is no safe ground, there are no automatic-pilot settings to carry us into a fully controlled landing. We must live with the risk, and discover in that risk the essence of our humanity and our daily excitement. Living with the ever-present possibility of crack-up is heavy stuff. But the possibility is real, and the only alternative to living with it is existing in ignorance or stupor.

"This is the best of all possible worlds," parroted Voltaire's Candide. But of course it isn't, and we cannot believe that it is, unless, at the same time, we are prepared to believe that even God has stopped working on it and has no further hope of its improvement.

Therefore we do the best we can with what we've got, and we study such things as the seasons of life—and where the bumps and

14

curves are likely to appear—in order to live as pleasantly and effectively as we can in the few short years we have. And we who are servants of the Word and the Sacraments even consider some of the special features of our particular life-order, in order that we may see ministry in a more meaningful perspective and thus adapt ourselves to it more efficaciously.

We will look first, in this series, at what it means to be young—young and impatient. Then we will explore what it means to be in early midlife, mired in professional busyness and threatened with the loss of personality. Third, we will examine what it means to terminate midlife and consider the final years of ministry. And finally, we will look at what it means to be retired in ministry, with time to review the efforts and effects of all the years preceding. There is crisis all along the way, as we have said, and particular crisis at the transition spots, when negotiation of one's way is everything and failure to negotiate can be disastrous.

What is the minister's help in all of this? Are we, who have counseled so many pilgrims along the torturous way of life, bereft of any special aid in the darker hours of our own journeying?

The answer to the question, of course, is the

same answer we offer to parishioners who seek our advice: *it is Christ.* There is not one remedy for one sort of person and another for the next. We are all engaged in the search for incarnation, for how the Spirit-stuff of the world and eternity can make lasting peace with the flesh-stuff, with the lower and more ephemeral forms of existence.

This was the apostle's concern in nearly every letter he wrote, and it came to a head in his great discussion of the works of the flesh and the fruits of the Spirit in Galatians 5. Unless we bring about incarnation, he said, we are mired in the products of the flesh on its own—in fornication, impurity, licentiousness, idolatry, sorcery, enmity, strife, jealousy, anger, selfishness, dissension, party spirit, envy, drunkenness, carousing, and the like. Talk about a list of life's crises! It is an inventory of the pastor's counseling subjects—and of what we all feel in our own lives when we are not successfully negotiating our personal journeys!

When we do bring about incarnation, said Paul, when Spirit has control of flesh, of the environment in which journeys are made, the fruits are opposite—love, joy, peace, patience, kindness, goodness, faithfulness, gentleness, self-control. You know that Spirit, don't you? You have felt it from time to time. Then is when ministry may be lived out of the overflow instead of the underflow, when it bubbles up and courses over the rim of life with spontaneity and joy.

So Christ, Spirit, incarnation, is the answer for us as well as for our people. And what we need to do, you and I, is to think about Christ again—Christ and our own lives, Christ and the seasons of our ministry. Then we shall aim toward the apostolic ideal of Christ in us, revealing the ineffable glory of God!

That is the purpose of these explorations—to consider what it means to be in Christ at the various junctures of our lives as ministers.

We are not all at the same place at the same time, of course, and so some of the explorations may be more meaningful to us in particular ways than others. But overall they will give us a sense of the panorama of ministry, and of how Christ is there in each segment to probe, invade, enliven, and renew us. And perhaps, with a feeling for the whole, we shall return to ministry with a new conviction for its meaning and purpose in our lives and in all of society.

To that end, we invoke the presence of the One who was crucified and raised from the dead, and we ask his blessings on all our thoughts and images, on all our words and ways.

# SPRING

## Learning to Wait for the Kingdom

When the days drew near for him to be received up, he set his face to go to Jerusalem. And he sent messengers ahead of him, who went and entered a village of the Samaritans, to make ready for him; but the people would not receive him, because his face was set toward Jerusalem. And when his disciples James and John saw it, they said, "Lord, do you want us to bid fire come down from heaven and consume them?" But he turned and rebuked them. And they went on to another village.

—LUKE 9:51–56

And when they came to the place which is called The Skull, there they crucified him, and the criminals, one on the right and one on the left. And Jesus said, "Father, forgive them; for they know not what they do."

—LUKE 23:33–34

In the beginning was the Word, and the Word was with God, and the Word was God. He was in the beginning with God; all things were made through him, and without him was not anything made that was made. In him was life, and the life was the light of men. The light shines in the darkness, and the darkness has not overcome it.

—JOHN 1:1–5

Call down fire out of heaven. It was the sort of thing young disciples might want to do. Scuttle the ship, block the pass, blow up the ungrateful so-and-sos! And therefore, says Mark, Jesus nicknamed James and John "Boanerges"—"sons of thunder." Or, if we follow Cranfill and others, sons of agitation and commotion.

It is a good nickname, chosen with a sense of humor. Thunder, not lightning—noisy but empty. Agitation and commotion—movement without progress. It is often descriptive of the first season of ministry, when enthusiasm is still running high and disappointments have not tempered the imagination. Now, of course, it would be sons *and daughters* of thunder—those who are full of fury at the world because it has only the sense of a backward-walking duck and has not surrendered itself to the Master. Sons and daughters of commotion, who hope to bring in the kingdom with programs and marches and boycotts!

I remember the night as if it were yesterday. I was a freshman at Baylor University, and had been asleep for two or three hours when I was roughly awakened by an excited friend. He was out of breath, having run all the way from town with the news. It was a distance of two or three miles, and he was not in shape for such exertions. He was so hysterical with fear and excitement that he broke into laughter several times while telling the story.

Earlier in the evening there had been a campus revival meeting. Feeling had run high, and there had been a caucus afterwards of eighteen or twenty ministerial candidates who thought the world should certainly be saved within the next thirty-six hours or their fervor had been in vain. Casting about for a suitable direction for their enthusiasm, they had quickly accepted someone's suggestion that they go down to the local sheriff's office, get themselves deputized, and go out with pickaxes and anything else they could find to break up all the houses of gambling and prostitution in the entire county.

Converging on the sheriff's office and discovering that he was not in at that hour of the evening, they had shifted about uneasily while waiting for his promised arrival. In the meantime, a Judas among them had slipped to a telephone booth and secretly called old Dr. Humphrey, the chairman of the university's religion department, to inform him of what was happening. Dr. Humphrey had stumbled into his trousers and arrived at the sheriff's office ahead of the sheriff, and he had threatened in blistering terms to cut off that very evening the tuition aid of every student who was not out of that office and back in his room in ten minutes.

My friend, who was hysterically narrating all of this to me, had heard this last while hanging by his fingers outside a window, whither he had retreated when he heard the news that Dr. Humphrey's car had been seen screeching to a halt outside the courthouse. He did not know anything more, as he had by then exhausted his prehensile ability and was forced to drop to the street, whence he had raced back to our rooming house without stopping for so much as a breath.

I was never quite certain whether his excitement was owing to the way Dr. Humphrey had foiled the adventure or to how close he had come to getting into a house of prostitution. But it was the sort of escapade most of us can recall from our salad days of ministry, when being sons and daughters of thunder didn't seem all that unusual.

There is an overweening confidence in the young, a kind of invincible optimism that they can remake the world in their generation. Graduates of Princeton may recall the bit of folklore from the days of John Mackay's presidency. Save-the-world fervor among fundamentalist students had risen to a high point, and some of them conceived a brilliant notion about how to proceed with the evangelization of their secular neighbor, the university, which was the only barrier standing between them and the conquest of the remainder of civilization. They would inscribe scripture verses on bits of paper, roll them tightly into little scrolls, tuck them into plastic pellets from the pharmacy, and then throw the pellets through all the open windows of the university dorms and classrooms. When Dr. Mackay heard about this plan, he stormed into chapel. "Boys," he said, with fire in his eyes and the sound of the earth splitting in his voice, "I know the Bible says we are to be fools for Christ; but, boys, it doesn't say 'damn fools'!"

If we smile at such hijinks, it is partly at ourselves, for only the most amnesiac among us cannot recall the damn-foolishness of his or her own early years in the ministry. They are almost always years of greenness, confidence, drive, pride, ambition, agitation, and commotion.

Blushing, I remember my own intemperateness. Johnny Killinger, evangelist. Greater than Sunday and Graham. Contemptuous of theologians, most of whom could not preach their way out of a wet Kleenex. Seer of angels, declarer of truth, architect of the new society. Purveyor of tracts to illiterate Negroes in the gin-bars of Texas cotton country. Once I routed from bed a white construction worker at eleven o'clock at night and converted him under the naked light bulb in the hall outside his apartment, while his almost-naked wife peered out the door in disbelieving curiosity. Another time I courageously broke into song from the pulpit, fatally wounding the enormously popular "It Is No Secret."

Perhaps I began to grow the winter's night I baptized twenty people by immersion in a borrowed church, standing in a borrowed rubber suit, and realized when I raised my arms from the pool for the benediction that I should have fastened the rubber cuffs as well, for water cascaded down my sleeves onto the wool trousers I would have to wear for the all-night trip back to my college. Thus God reminds us of the earthenness of our vessels, and brings us back to "low dō," as my departed mother-in-law liked to put it.

A scholar named Martin Light has written a book called *The Quixotic Vision of Sinclair Lewis.* That is what it is with us, isn't it—our quixotic vision, our Don Quixote way of seeing the world and ourselves, of dramatizing our callings, tilting at windmills, and rescuing people in distress. Things appear so simple and straightforward when we are young. Christ seems so imminent, the problems so obvious, the solutions so clear, the victory so attainable.

We have only to throw ourselves into the breach
and the eschaton will come. The trumpets will
sound, the skies will darken, Christ will descend,
and we ourselves will have been the compelling
factor, the *sine qua non* for which the world
was waiting—indeed, for which all creation
groaned from the beginning until now.

Ah, sweet mystery of life! The tender dreams
of the young. The beauty of innocence. And
somehow, over the years, we survive our own
beginnings, grow out of them as the tall corn
grows from the tiny, vulnerable blades that first
appear in the soil. We survive, and we wonder
whatever happened to the blue skies and starlit
nights of youth, the energy and ambition and
unbridled enthusiasm, the drive and devotion
and marvelous decisiveness.

Youth is a wonderful season of life, but most
of us who have survived would not wish to go
back and live it again. Why? Could it be because
we now know something of the long plan of
God, the slow winning of the kingdom, the
patient waiting for the corn to grow up—and
the squash and tomatoes and kumquats as well?
Because our youth embarrasses us, and we
prefer the maturer vision of middle life and
beyond?

# SPRING

There was an article years ago, in the *Atlantic Monthly* I think, about a little burro that was employed, in the heyday of the great western cattle ranches, to gentle the strongest steers. The steer, bucking and convulsing like a raging sailor, was haltered to the little burro, and the two together turned loose, Laurel and Hardy, onto the desert range. They would be seen disappearing over the horizon, the great steer tossing the poor burro about like a streamer in the wind. They would sometimes be gone for days. But eventually they would return, the little burro in the lead, trotting along for home with the submissive steer in tow. Somewhere, out on the rim of the world, the steer would become exhausted from his strenuous attempts to rid himself of the burro; and at that point the burro would take mastery and become the leader.

Thus it is with the kingdom and its heroes in the long plan of God. The battle is to the determined, not the outraged, the committed, not the dramatic. Stand sometime on the stone ramparts of Mont Saint Michel or in the cool nave of Winchester Cathedral. Breathe the air of the centuries and think of the timelessness of faith waiting for the end. Remember how long God has been at work on these playthings of eternity. Then regard the ardor and ambition of youth and utter the words of the Preacher, "Vanity of vanities! All is vanity" (Eccl. 1:2).

That's why the smile is on the sphinx, isn't it? The sphinx is thinking about the young—all of those under a thousand years old.

Don't misunderstand. I am not debunking youth and its enthusiasms. God give us more of both. But God also pardon us for them.

Jesus called youthful disciples, among others, and apparently he felt more attachment to young John—the teenager?—than to any of the others. But he also rebuked their eagerness to destroy their enemies, to have the kingdom in a cocked hat (see Luke 9:51–56). Why? Because they weren't always able to tell their enemies from their friends, or vice versa? Because their enemies were sometimes inside themselves?

Wouldn't this passage in which Jesus rebukes the disciples have been a perfect place for the author to have set the parable of the wheat and the tares? Let them grow up together. Be patient. Wait. Because otherwise you tear up the good with the evil, and destroy the valuable with that which has no value.

It is not easy, is it, learning to be patient, to see the world with God's ancient eyes and then to wait a while longer? Or to be like Jesus on the cross, blessing one's enemies and crowning their worst efforts with forgiveness. Not easy at all. To the young it seems like failure. "Why didn't you smash them when you had the chance?" "What good is power if you don't use it?" Pickaxes in the houses of prostitution.

But there is mystery here, in the word of forgiveness from the instrument of torture. Perhaps *the* mystery, or at least the point where mystery touches us most intimately. "Forgive them." Not blind rage, but "Forgive them." Not fire out of heaven, but "Forgive them." Not a nuclear holocaust, but "Forgive them." The secret of secrets, to be reviled and not revile in return, to hurt and not respond with passion. Mystery in a nutshell. A new way of seeing the world—and one's enemies—and the grace of God at work in it all.

That is what we have to come to see when we are young, and what we have to do. We have to learn to love. And oh, it is so hard and takes so long for love really to become love and not mere rhetoric, for love to be caring—deep, genuine caring—and not concern for one's own posture or image.

Churchill, said Lord Atlee, had a way of standing back to look at himself and his country

as he believed the world and its history would.
"He was always, in effect, asking himself, 'How
will I look if I do this or that?' " Love doesn't
do that. Love isn't concerned for PR and images.
Love embraces the world like an old parent who
long ago gave up worrying about self. Love
empties itself in its care for the other. That is
the word from the cross—a word of patience
and tolerance and knowing that in the long haul
it is God who brings in the kingdom, not we
ourselves.

I heard a father reminiscing about his
children. He had torn down an old shed that
had stood on the family property for years and
years. His children had played in it when they
were young, and then it had fallen into ill repair
and he was just getting around to taking it down.
In its dismantling he had discovered, under the
rotten old floorboards, a deck of cards and some
old cigarette packages. Both cards and cigarettes
had been forbidden for children in those stricter
times, and here was the evidence of their
humanity, uncovered after all those years. The
father was laughing about it. Then, he would
have raged like a stuck bull. Now, it is part of
the humor of life—something to smile about,
even to treasure.

And so it is with age. It helps us to love and to care, and to smile with indulgence at the little things that don't matter.

One thing is sure: we know, when we get older, that we won't change the world the way we thought we would when we were young. The sons and daughters of thunder may not become the fathers and mothers of whimper, but we know how deeply etched into the nature of the world some things are, and we stop straining to move the immovable. Even the beloved disciple learned this, and from being a son of agitation or commotion became (we think) the author of a Gospel of love and confidence in the power of God to complete the work God has begun in Christ Jesus. We picture him at the end as placid and undisturbed, his eyes resting calmly on a future that works itself out without the feverish and spasmodic assistance of the young Turks who think it will arrive tomorrow.

It just may be that we are not called to change everything in the world but to love it; and, in the loving, it may change.

Browsing in a London bookstall, I happened upon an old volume by Mrs. Leslie Stephens called *Notes from Sick Rooms.* It was a book

of instructions for domestic nurses. My eye fell
upon this passage:

> When an illness has gone on for some time the
> sick person becomes very weary of the things
> which surround her. She has looked at all the
> pictures which hang on the walls, and at the
> patterns which ornament or disfigure the paper,
> till she can bear them no longer. The nurse cannot,
> of course, alter all these things, but she can give
> a certain change to the aspect of the room. A
> looking-glass so placed that it can reflect the sky
> and trees, or, if the sufferer is in London, some
> portion of the street, will be a refreshment to the
> eyes which have for long not pierced beyond the
> narrow boundary of the sick room.*

The older pastor will recognize in these words
something central to the business of ministry.
We cannot remake the world in which our
people live, despite all our youthful ambitions.
In fact, one of the persistent ingredients of
despair over the years will have been a sense
of inadequacy to effect any great changes at all.
But one learns, in the course of living, how to
work with the looking-glass to make things more

* Republished Bradley, ME: Puckerworth Press, 1980, p. 31.

bearable for those who suffer—to reveal to them new vistas, perspectives they have never seen, ways of looking at the world for the first time since they were children. And who knows but that, in the course of making the world look new, it actually becomes new, and moves closer to the kingdom?

What John learned, you see, what the tempestuous boy came to see as he lived longer in discipleship, was that the newness lies in wait, and one doesn't always provoke its appearance by strong-arm tactics, by storming the citadels and brandishing pickaxes, but by enticing it with love and gentleness and assurances of unity. We don't make the world over by calling down fire from heaven; we do it by being there when people need us, when the crisis in life occurs and they are at a flashpoint of learning and seeing.

Like Dot McGehee, a fifty-five-year-old woman in my parish who became terminally ill with cancer of the lungs. "I want to learn how to die," she said on my second visit in the hospital. "Will you help me?" I had preached about death and dying and the afterlife many times, but she had not been able to hear. Now she knew she was staring into the deep shadows, and she was ready to learn. We remake the world, my friends, by being there when they are ready, by waiting in love just as the new world is waiting to be born.

And then the God of all readiness says "Now!," and a world springs into being!

# Prayer

Praise be to you, O God,
for youth and ambition and enthusiasm.
But enable us to survive them, we pray,
in order to enter more deeply into
the mystery of your love and patience.
Teach us to see your glory in a
raindrop on a leaf,
and in the eyes of a child,
as much as in the spires of cathedrals
and throngs of mindless converts.
Through Jesus Christ our Lord,
AMEN.

# SUMMER

Finding the Strength
to Serve

*The apostles returned to Jesus, and told him all that they had done and taught. And he said to them, "Come away by yourselves to a lonely place, and rest a while." For many were coming and going, and they had no leisure even to eat. And they went away in the boat to a lonely place by themselves. Now many saw them going, and knew them, and they ran there on foot from all the towns, and got there ahead of them. As he went ashore he saw a great throng, and he had compassion on them, because they were like sheep without a shepherd; and he began to teach them many things. And when it grew late, his disciples came to him and said, "This is a lonely place, and the hour is now late; send them away, to go into the country and villages round about and buy themselves something to eat." But he answered them, "You give them something to eat." And they said to him, "Shall we go and buy two hundred denarii worth of bread, and give it to them to eat?" And he said to them, "How many loaves have you? Go and see." And when they had found out, they said, "Five, and two fish." Then he commanded them all to sit down by companies upon the green grass. So they sat down in groups, by hundreds and by fifties. And taking the five loaves and the two fish he looked up to heaven, and blessed, and broke the loaves, and gave them to the disciples to set before the people; and he divided the two fish among them all. And they all ate and were satisfied. And they took up twelve baskets full of broken pieces and of the fish. And those who ate the loaves were five thousand men.*

—MARK 6:30–44

Send them away."

Boy, I know the feeling, don't you?

Life in the fish bowl.

"Send them away."

Life in the *piranha* bowl. People always taking little pieces of you. A little bit here and a little bit there. Pretty soon there's nothing left of you but a stain in the water.

All that energy going out.

"Who touched me?" asked Jesus (Mark 5:30, Luke 9:45). He could feel it going out.

So do we.
Touch.
Touch.
Touch.
And eventually we feel depleted, worn out, exhausted. Nothing left to go on with. All periphery and no center.

"Send them away."

My wife, bless her, knows how to do it. We had been in our new pastorate ten months when a dear lady, well meaning, called up to speak of another lady, not so well meaning, who was bad-mouthing the pastor because he had not yet called on her mother. (Actually he had, and the poor lady in her senility could never remember it.) "Tell her to phone me," said my wife; "there are two things I would like to say to her." "Oh?" oh-h-ed the voice on the line. "Yes," said my wife. "First, John is not God, and, second, stuff it!" There was a fluttering noise on the other end of the line, as if a canary had just fallen off its perch into the birdseed, and I have not heard another word of criticism in the parish.

"Send them away."

The disciples were out there in the wilderness setting, needing to be alone with the Master, and all those people followed them. "Rabbi, this eye is diseased." "Rabbi, this knee doesn't bend properly." "Rabbi, I don't hear so well out of this ear." "Rabbi, what did you mean about 'rendering unto Caesar's what is Caesar's'?" "Rabbi, this" and "Rabbi, that." Sometimes it was enough to make one want to demit the rabbinate!

You know the feeling.

"Send them away."

It is especially characteristic of the middle years of ministry—the *successful* years, if you please—when most ministers have graduated from their two- and three-point charges of earlier years, when they have their names printed on the bulletin boards in more than chalk, and on liturgical bulletins with a high rag content (maybe even with feathered edges), and are called on to commencerate high schools and sit on the boards and agencies of the greater church. It is then, in these years, that the appointment book gets to look like a telephone directory with every space filled, that people pick the most inconsiderate times to die and your most influential members elect to have their operations in hospitals fifty miles away, that there is always some staff position to be filled, with letters and tapes and interviews and meetings, and all of it growing exponentially until it threatens to take over everything like the incredible kudzu vine. During these years committees become such a constant fixture of life that you wake up at night from some Kafkaesque dream, convinced that you are condemned to spending the rest of your life inside an agenda that is written in Arabic or Sanskrit. And the preparation of great sermons, the ones that were going to land you in G. Paul Butler's books (dear old G. Paul), is reduced to an inspiration while shaving, an outline concocted between hospitals, and a couple of illustrations poorly recalled from last year's general conference.

What a pity, to be successful!

I shall never forget standing with Tom Shipp, the great founding pastor of Lover's Lane United Methodist Church in Dallas, in his cluttered study beside the busy Northwest Highway that ran just outside. "Tom," I remonstrated, "why in the world, with all these sixteen acres of land to build your campus on, did you put your study here by that infernal traffic?!" Tom was quiet for a moment. He stood with his hands behind his back, thoughtfully regarding the constant flow of cars and trucks.

"Sometimes," he said, "I just like to stand here and watch something moving that I didn't have to push."

"Send them away."

The shame is that we become robots—mechanical people, going through the motions of ministry. The clerical mask is there—by the sickbed, in the counseling session, behind the pulpit, by the graveside—but the face behind it grows more and more passionless, more and more anonymous. Work, because it is demanding and relentless, becomes routine. The edges of personhood are ground off. We come to the dinner table and stare, as the discussion ebbs and flows around us. Our children grow up and we wonder when it happened. Our wives or husbands grow old alone, companionless as herons in the twilight.

It was there in the last sermon a friend of mine gave before he left his church—the note of sadness and emptiness that preceded news of his and his wife's separation. "I have been like a pump beside the road," he said, "with a sign on it that said to everyone passing by, 'I am here for you. Take my handle and pump me and slake your thirst.' " And gradually, he said, he had been pumped dry. There wasn't anything life-giving left for him. He didn't have any time for his family or himself.

"Send them away."

But Jesus didn't do it, did he? He didn't send them away.

Instead, he had the disciples seat everybody— five thousand of them, by ministerial estimate. He blessed the little that the disciples had and made it enough to feed all of them abundantly, with enough left over to put in the freezer for the next picnic. And then a short time later, according to the eighth chapter of Mark, he did the same trick again and fed four thousand people, with more food for the freezer.

Bread for the wilderness.

That was it, wasn't it? Jesus was the master of wilderness places. He came up with the bread when they needed it. Mark brings the point home over there in the eighth chapter. Jesus and the disciples were out in a boat after the two feeding miracles, and they had forgotten to bring any fresh bread with them. There was one loaf in the boat, probably tucked under a seat days before, wrapped in somebody's old sweatshirt, crusty and stale. And the disciples, realizing they had forgotten to bring any new bread, fell to whispering among themselves.

"Didn't you bring it?"

"No, I thought you were going to."

"It was Philip's responsibility this time. I brought it last time."

"What'll we do?"

And Jesus, says Mark, perceiving what they were talking about, said, "You foolish children! How long must I be with you before you understand? How many basketsful of leftovers did you pick up back there when we fed five thousand people?"

"Twelve."

"Right. And how many when we fed the four thousand?"

"Seven," sheepishly.

"For shame! You have eyes, can't you see? You have ears, can't you hear? Where is your sense of understanding?"

The master of all bread production was in the boat with them, and they were worrying about a few loaves for their own use.

Is this what Paul was talking about over in Galatians when he spoke of the indwelling Christ, and of Christ being formed in us, and of walking by the Spirit, and of the fruits of the Spirit being love, joy, peace, patience, kindness, goodness, faithfulness, gentleness, self-control?

Isn't it all about having something in the pump, even after everybody has had hold of the pump handle and has worked it for all it was worth? That's the trick, isn't it, to be able to give and give and give and still have something left over to live out of?

Jesus took the disciples out into a lonely place to be alone with him. He took them out in a boat to be alone with him. They prayed out there in those places. They thought about the kingdom and about what its coming meant to them and to all the people around them. They got in touch with the Holy at the centers of their beings, so that something was happening to the way they looked at things. They were being converted to the way Jesus thought and behaved and went about the business of living. They were with Jesus, and he fed them.

Does any of this have implications for ministry?

"Send them away."

"No, we will feed them."

Christ and you. Christ and me. Christ and us, if you will forgive the emphatic bad grammar.

Our problem is that we run dry, don't we? The energy goes, the pump gives out, the bread is exhausted, because we get so busy supplying everybody's needs that we forget our own; we neglect the lonely places with Christ; we fail to get refilled with the Spirit. The piranha get all there is, and there is only a stain in the water.

Let's not pretend, with each other or ourselves.

Ministry is a lonely place without Christ.

Ministry is exhausting without Christ.

Ministry is impossible without Christ.

Feeding on him is the only way to make it through middlescence in the ministry. It is the only way to find strength to serve.

Johann Sebastian Bach understood. He wasn't a minister in the same sense that we are, but he had to produce and produce endlessly as a Christian musician. It was like being a preacher in a world-renowned pulpit, unable to let down a single Sunday without setting the tongues to wagging. And on almost all of his manuscripts Bach placed two sets of initials. At the end he wrote the letters, "S.D.G." and, at the beginning, "J.J." S.D.G., *Soli deo gloria*—to God alone be the glory. And J.J., *Jesu juvet*—Jesus, help me.

We could do worse than inscribe the same initials at the beginning and ending of each day of ministry. At the end, S.D.G., "To God alone be the glory." And, at the beginning, J.J., "Jesus, help me."

Jesus, help me.

But what if he isn't there?

What if the pump is dry?

I have a dear friend for whom it was dry. His name is Wayne Pipkin. When I met Wayne a number of years ago he was a professor of church history at a large university. He was a splendid man, and much beloved by his students. But something happened, and Wayne didn't get tenure. He and Arlene had to sell the beautiful little pink brick house they had built a few blocks from the campus.

Wayne looked long and hard for a job, but church historian positions were scarce as the proverbial hen's teeth. For a while it looked as if Arlene might have to take their two little girls and go to live with her parents while Wayne traveled from city to city seeking work. Then, as if by grace, a position opened for Wayne in Columbus, Ohio; he would be director of a seminary consortium. It was not the job he had hoped for, but it was a means of keeping his family together. So he and Arlene bought another little house in Columbus and settled in again to raising their daughters.

A year or two later, lightning struck again. Wayne learned that the seminary consortium was folding and that he would once more be without work. The trauma of the first experience came back upon him, deepening his gloom over the second one. There didn't seem to be work anywhere. The outlook was bleak. Wayne fell into depression. He had trouble eating and sleeping. Friends feared a breakdown.

While despondency reigned, Wayne turned desperately to an attempt to renew his neglected prayer life. One of his discoveries was of an ancient method, practiced by St. Ignatius and his monks, of fantasizing a relaxing scene, putting themselves in it, and permitting God to lead the action from there.

Wayne thought of one of his favorite places. Since seminary days in Hartford, Connecticut, he had loved the rockbound coast of northern New England. Trying to relax, he pictured himself walking along that coast on a warm, sunny day in June. The heat felt good through his shirt, and soon he felt his muscles becoming free and less tense. It was a beautiful day, and he thought he could smell the wonderful salt air as it filled his lungs. Gulls were flying overhead, calling out to one another as they dropped shellfish on the rocks below.

Soon Wayne felt so good that when he saw a path leading down the cliff to the rocks below he took it, and was soon climbing over the stones at the very edge of the water. Then he saw a bottle floating in the edge of the tide, and could see that there was a message rolled up inside. Instinctively, he knew the message was for him! It was something God wanted to say to him at this stressful time of his life. He must have the bottle! Wading out into the surf a few feet, he rescued the bobbing container, and had soon thrust his finger inside and retrieved the little scroll. He was tingling with excitement, because he knew it was God's word for him.

*Hodie christus natus est.*

That was the message, in Latin.

*Hodie christus natus est.*

"Today, Christ is born."

Wayne was crestfallen. He had expected some important message for him. Not *Hodie christus natus est.* His life was on the rocks. He felt wrung out, dry, exhausted, unable to go on. He wanted to know what was going to happen to him and his family. He wanted to know where to turn for a job. And there was that impertinent message, *Hodie christus natus est.* Something he had known all his life, almost; since he was a boy, at least.

Or had he?

As he thought about it, and tried to pray, Wayne realized it was a message he had forgotten. He might have known it, but it had gotten crowded out in his busy, desperate life. Now, in his hour of great need, it had come back as gospel, as Good News. "Today Christ is born." And it happened inside Wayne. The indwelling Christ returned, and he began walking in the Spirit again. All his fears and anxieties, all his concerns about life and livelihood, moved to the periphery again, out of the center, so that the Spirit could live at the center.

Eventually Wayne did find a job. He is now a professor of church history at a seminary in Rüschlikon, Switzerland. He and Arlene and their daughters are supremely happy there, for they thrive in the international setting.

But that is not the important thing.

The important thing is that Christ, who had not been at the center of Wayne's life, had come back. And even if there had been no job, if he had never been able to teach again, Wayne had found a peace and joy beyond all understanding.

"Send them away?"
No.
Demit the ministry?
No.
Find the center again. Live out of the center
Out of the Spirit.
Has he been so long with us and we don't
understand?

# Prayer

We are nothing without you, O Lord,
and it is hard to be something
when one is nothing.
It is hard to keep moving,
hard to keep pumping,
hard to keep giving out,
without you.
Come back to our lives in strength.
Renew the Spirit within us.
Give us bread for our wildernesses.
For you are the Christ,
the Son of the Living God.
AMEN.

# FALL

## Accepting Our Failures

And in the fourth watch of the night he came to them, walking on the sea. But when the disciples saw him walking on the sea, they were terrified, saying, "It is a ghost!" And they cried out for fear. But immediately he spoke to them, saying, "Take heart, it is I; have no fear." And Peter answered him, "Lord, if it is you, bid me come to you on the water." He said, "Come." So Peter got out of the boat and walked on the water and came to Jesus; but when he saw the wind, he was afraid, and beginning to sink he cried out, "Lord, save me." Jesus immediately reached out his hand and caught him, saying to him, "O man of little faith, why did you doubt?" And when they got into the boat, the wind ceased. And those in the boat worshiped him, saying, "Truly you are the Son of God."

—MATTHEW 14:25–33

Then they seized him and led him away, bringing him into the high priest's house. Peter followed at a distance; and when they had kindled a fire in the middle of the courtyard and sat down together, Peter sat among them. Then a maid, seeing him as he sat in the light and gazing at him, said, "This man also was with him." But he denied it, saying, "Woman, I do not know him."

—LUKE 22:54–57

When they had finished breakfast, Jesus said to Simon Peter, "Simon, son of John, do you love me more than these?" He said to him, "Yes, Lord; you know that I love you." He said to him, "Feed my lambs." A second time he said to him, "Simon, son of John, do you love me?"

He said to him, "Yes, Lord; you know that I love you."
He said to him, "Tend my sheep." He said to him the
third time, "Simon, son of John, do you love me?" Peter
was grieved because he said to him the third time, "Do
you love me?" And he said to him, "Lord, you know
everything; you know that I love you." Jesus said to him,
"Feed my sheep."

—JOHN 21:15–17

I assume that the "fall" of Peter in the story of walking on water is transhistorical, that it is for the right-brained and image-minded among us an artist's rendering of what really happened that night in Gethsemane and later in the courtyard of the high priest. That is, it represents Peter's actual fall from faith, the moment when he saw soldiers marching by torchlight, forgot all about the kingdom, whipped out his sword, and began flailing through a nightmare of high seas and denials. But Jesus, unwilling that this dear man be lost forever beneath the waves, reached out and helped him back into the boat, reclaiming him from his fear of soldiers. And walking with him arm and arm (was it by the same sea where he was represented as falling?), Jesus gently but firmly reminded him, "Feed my sheep."

I also assume that this is something that can happen to every one of us—and indeed does, at some point of ministry. It is part of what breaks down the *hubris,* the unmitigated pride, of the youthful minister and changes, as if by transubstantiation, enthusiasm into patience for the kingdom of God. And, as part of the developmental cycle of the minister's life, it is most likely to happen during the difficult transition period from early to later middle age, when the minister is smack in the middle of reassessing his or her pilgrimage and deciding where it is likely to lead in the years that are left.

"I am convinced," says Peter Chew in his book, *The Inner World of the Middle-Aged Man,* "that man's search at midlife is ultimately a spiritual one." And Richard Olson, to whom I am indebted for that quotation, adds this word from Carl Jung, the great psychoanalyst: "Among all my patients in the second half of life—that is to say, over thirty-five—there has not been one whose problem in the last resort was not that of finding a religious outlook on life."

It is general, not particular; it happens to all, not only to ministers; and it is natural, with ministers as with others, for the breakdown or fall or reassessment to occur in terms of the spiritual pilgrimage.

What we are doing, you see, after the period of intense activity and achievement that characterizes early middle life, is stopping to reexamine the course we are on, and to decide whether the trip has been worth it. For some, this means coming to terms with the failure to achieve—with having spent all those years in the search for the Holy Grail, only to come up weary and exhausted with full realization that it is too late, that they will never find the Grail. Or, even worse, it means coming to suspect that there is no Grail at all.

I have a friend who is about due for that. He is a Southern Baptist with all the unbridled ambition that sometimes characterizes young ministers in that convention. From age fifteen to forty, he has been possessed by a dream of ministerial greatness. For years he has sent out an annual letter listing all his accomplishments that year: "Preached 313 times, published 87 articles, spoke on TV 23 times, visited mission fields in 17 countries, etc." It is all puff, of course. He manages to continue from year to year in the hope that some of it will one day come true. But now he is nearing the time when he must admit that it will not, that the Grail is unattainable, that his goals for himself and his ministry were not consonant with his personality and abilities. In short, he must cope with his failure, as many of us must in midlife.

The alternative is to cope with success. That too can be a sad story.

I think of another minister, one who has surely fulfilled all his life's ambitions and then some. For several years he has been pastor of a large, prestigious church—you know the kind, one with stained glass even in the bathrooms, and cloth towels to wipe your hands on. He is known as the "bishop" of his community. I asked him a few months ago to speak of the thoughts that run through his mind as he enters the last phase of his ministry. "Sex and love," he said. Sex and love.

"I've had a devil of a time with sex these last few years," he said. "Wanta put my arm around every attractive woman I see. Put my arm around her—hell, I want to get into bed with her. I haven't. But I've sure had the urge."

"By love," he said, "I mean this." He waved his hand in a semi-sweep, indicating the extremely large church building completed within the last five years. "I used to think that the ultimate was to build this building. You know, the old edifice complex. Now that it's built, I think a lot about love. What good is a building if the people aren't changed? I'd like to spend the rest of my ministry teaching people how to love. If they don't learn . . ." His words trailed off in another gesture, a gesture of partial hopelessness, as if he didn't know if he could pull it off, as if his glorious success as a builder was somehow fatally flawed by his discovery too late that love is the goal of everything.

Maybe the sex angle wasn't as unrelated to this as seems apparent. For years, the building had been the important thing, an erection in stone and mortar. Then, when the success of that was called into question, real sex came back with a vengeance—the *élan vital,* the life force, surging back where it had been denied. It often happens with people in late midlife. They want to make up for lost time, to touch flesh, to be real as "ordinary people" are real.

## FALL

What was it someone wrote about childhood
and old age?

> You will not see the world at first:
> You will touch flesh and you will cry.
> Years later you will cry because
> You see too much and touch too little.*

Maybe my friend feared he had missed
something on the way to his success story,
something other people were finding and taking
for granted.

Henry Ward Beecher did the same thing at
midlife. He was riding the crest of enormous
popularity, friend of President Lincoln,
celebrated preacher and author, renowned
traveler, idol of thousands, if not millions. And
then it came out in a trial that he had risked
it all—the popularity, the riches, the
idolization—for the affection of two women in
his congregation at Plymouth Church. He had
even come to confuse his love for them with
spirituality, for, as Jung implied, that is what
we are seeking in midlife, wherever we look
for it.

---

* Edwin Brock, "D-Day Minus," *The Listener* (London), 28
November 1963.

## Accepting Our Failures

What is failure and what success in ministry? That is the thorny part, isn't it? Sometimes we fail for having aimed at the wrong kind of success, and maybe, if it has helped us to avoid that pitfall, we can even conceive of failure as a kind of success. It is like the man who thanks God he was never any kind of ladies' man, else he would have been a *debauché*, for that was ever his inclination.

It is all confusing, especially when you are midway in the stream of life and trying to sort it all out. And sometimes the confusion leads people to cash in their chips, valueless as they are, and leave the ministry, hoping for some remaining life in an "honest" profession.

Like one friend of mine, who finally had enough of his own weakness as a leader and as a preacher, as well as enough of his unwilling helpmeet of a wife. He divorced the church and his wife in the same week, slinking off to remarry and seek fulfillment in another kind of work.

Or like Shannon, in Tennessee Williams' *Night of the Iguana,* who stood in his pulpit drunk one Sunday morning and told his whitely starched congregation, all aghast, what they could do with their pusillanimous faith and the anemic little God who went with it.

# FALL

It is all Simon Peter falling beneath the waves and flailing out madly in an effort at salvaging something of the self.

Robert Raines put it beautifully in his little book *Going Home*, which was his *nunc dimittis*, his *apologia* for having done what Shannon did—telling off his father (who was a hero-bishop in the church) and his wife as well, forsaking a five-thousand-member church in Columbus, Ohio for a new and frightening leg of his pilgrimage. Describing Leonard Bernstein's *Mass*, Raines says:

The celebrant who is Every Man has robe after robe laid on him by others or by himself. Layer upon layer of expectation go over him—the constraints of obligation—until he literally staggers under the burden of all those investments laid on him. Finally, driven to extremity, in a wild and frightening scene he literally tears off the vestments, layer after layer, turning, twisting, ripping, stretching, until he stands clear and free before the altar, divested in the presence of the people under God. He has ripped off his own grave clothes to become vulnerable and real in the world.*

* (San Franciso: Harper & Row, Pub., 1979), p. 39.

That is strong, isn't it? We feel the emotion in it, throbbing and burning.

Is the remedy always this radical? Must it be? Does the hand of Christ that helps us into the boat always lead first to the far country?

I am thinking of another testing, another temperament. Gerald Forshee is the film critic for *The Christian Century*. Do you remember the editorial he wrote in the *Century* after his house had been burglarized?

The Forshees had elected a long time before to remain in the inner city of Chicago and not join the white flight to the suburbs. They wanted to stand for reconciliation and love in a neighborhood that was learning more and more about hate and *apartheid*. Then somebody knocked over their house—entered and ransacked, violated its sanctity. The Forshees came home and were sick at the discovery. They felt raped, betrayed, defeated. Their first impulse, said Forshee, was to flee the place, to get out, to pack it all in and say, "Forget this business; we've paid long enough!" But then they cooled down and thought about it and decided to stay. After all, their contract hadn't promised a bed of roses.

Finally, after sharing all of this in his editorial,

Forshee concluded by paraphrasing a popular religious song of the fifties, "It Is No Secret." "It is no secret," he wrote, "what God can do. What He's done to Jesus, He'll do to you." And they stayed.

The circumstances were different, of course, and the Forshees were different people. It isn't the same with all of us, and we should never sit in judgment on those who take a way we would not take. But it is still the story of Simon Peter and the engulfing waves. Whether our doubt and hesitance are for a moment or for ten years, we say no to Christ—or at least, "Wait a minute, Jesus, I'm not so sure about this any more." We can't help it. It's simply the way things are when you're forty or fifty and the road you were on suddenly comes to a washout, or else to a multiple forking where every road looks more promising than the one you were on.

The effect personally seems devastating. After all the years, all the discipleship, all the pastoring and preaching, to hit the soft shoulder of doubt, to feel the waves parting beneath your feet and have that sense of spiritual vertigo or emotional queasiness that comes with it—"Lord, who can stand?"

It is part of what Paul calls walking in the flesh, in the power of our own momentum, and not in the Spirit. The works of the flesh, he says, are plain: "fornication, gross indecency and sexual irresponsibility; idolatry and sorcery; feuds and wrangling, jealousy, bad temper and quarrels; disagreements, factions, envy; drunkenness, orgies, and similar things" (Gal. 5:19–21, JB). This is not a complete catalogue of the works of the flesh but an illustrative list. When we try to walk in our own strength, these are what we get. Idolatry, even—the worship of little gods, not *the* God. Maybe they're the sign of tiredness in the ministry, of having had enough, of having been in the piranha bowl too long. Or maybe they are the sign of not having been living in the Presence, being indwelled by the Spirit, for the fruits of the Spirit are the opposite: love, joy, peace, patience, gentleness, self-control.

That's it, isn't it? Another turning point in life, another transition period; and the only thing that saves us from going under the waves is the outstretched hand of the Master. "Here, child, get in the boat." "Here, son, daughter, there are more sheep to feed."

Christ is the answer, no matter how much

we dislike the cliché. There isn't another. John
the Baptist's followers asked, "Are you the one,
or look we for another?" And Jesus answered,
"Go tell John what you have seen, how the lame
walk and the blind see and the deaf hear." It's
the same for us: "Look back across your ministry.
Think of all you've seen. What other answer
could there be?"

Did you read Robert McAfee Brown's spiritual
autobiography, *Creative Dislocation—The
Movement of Grace?* What a powerful man!
What a ministry he has had! What freshness he
has continued to bring to his calling year after
year, theme after theme, movement after
movement! Cleverly, he begins the book with
a series of "snapshots" or moments from his life,
word-pictures designed to elicit the times he
has been through. Sacramental moments, for,
as he says, "In a sacrament, life is for a single
moment the way it is supposed to be in all
moments." Several of the snapshots are of his
wife and children—Peter, Mark, Alison, Tom—
sometimes with their guitars, sometimes in
protest lines, once leaping for joy when LBJ said
he would not seek reelection, and once together
at Christmas. "There we all are," says Brown,
"gathered around the crèche on Christmas Eve,

putting the animals and the wise men and the shepherds around the baby who is a small center of sanity in a large and crazy world." Beautiful! A small center of sanity in a large and crazy world. Who could put it better? What other answer could there be?

So we turn back again (like Yeats' "rough beast slouching toward Bethlehem to be born"?), like old Simon Peter, asking forgiveness for the denials and finding reinstatement in ministry for the time that is left. Wanting sheep to feed. Ready to lead them by still waters and into green pastures, for his name's sake. Wanting the love, joy, and peace that come from walking in the Spirit, from being indwelled by the Spirit.

And who knows, maybe the end will be better than the beginning! Maybe faith will take hold even more strongly than before. That would be something, wouldn't it?

Frederick W. Robertson found it that way. One of the greatest of the great. Head and shoulders among most of his contemporaries, yet never seeming to notice. Died at thirty-seven, prematurely old and worn, his body racked with pain. He was stuff of our stuff: overworked, underpaid, the target of many accusations from both church members and strangers because he dared to side with working people. He didn't even trust the popularity that came to him. This great man was always troubled by hidden thoughts of failure, depressed on Sunday evenings by a feeling he had not done well. He said he could hardly bear the degradation of being a Brighton preacher. Yet in one of the loneliest times of his life he wrote, "I read Shakespeare, Wordsworth, Tennyson, Coleridge, Philip Van Artevelde, for views of man to meditate upon, instead of theological caricatures of humanity; and I go into the country to *feel* God; dabble in chemistry, to feel awe of Him; read the life of Christ, to understand, love, and adore Him; and my experience is closing into this, that I turn with disgust from everything to Christ."

Ponder that, will you? "I turn with disgust from everything to Christ." So Raines and Forshee. So Simon Peter. So all of us. In the end, what else is there? After the stormy night at sea or the toilsome night with no fish taken, we come in to the Christ of the open fire, with the fish quietly simmering in a pan, and feel again the excitement that has grabbed at our hearts all these years, ever since we were youngsters. We walk with him along the shore, skipping rocks and thinking of faraway places, and hear him ask, probing gently, "Do you love me?"

"Yes, Lord, you know I do."

"Feed my sheep."

You can resist a scene like that? I can't.

"I turn with disgust from everything to Christ."

Maybe not quite with disgust. But I know what he means.

There isn't any comparison.

# Prayer

It is in finding Christ, Lord,
that we find the world and ourselves.
Reach out to us now,
in our stormy situations,
and take us by the hand.
Bring us back to the boat with
new commitment,
new insight,
new energy.
For yours is the gift of *life*.
AMEN.

# WINTER

Looking Forward to God

*I have fought the good fight, I have finished the race, I have kept the faith. Henceforth there is laid up for me the crown of righteousness, which the Lord, the righteous judge, will award to me on that Day, and not only to me but also to all who have loved his appearing.*

—2 TIMOTHY 4:7–8


*But whatever gain I had, I counted as loss for the sake of Christ. Indeed I count everything as loss because of the surpassing worth of knowing Christ Jesus my Lord. For his sake I have suffered the loss of all things, and count them as refuse, in order that I may gain Christ and be found in him, not having a righteousness of my own, based on law, but that which is through faith in Christ, the righteousness from God that depends on faith; that I may know him and the power of his resurrection, and may share his sufferings, becoming like him in his death, that if possible I may attain the resurrection from the dead.*

—PHILIPPIANS 3:7–11

Retirement is a modern phenomenon.
Fifty years ago, almost nobody retired.
Can you imagine the apostle Paul in
retirement? He would have been like a
Methodist preacher I heard about who was so
nervous that he wore his suits out from the
inside. Can you imagine *any* of the apostles in
retirement? John, maybe, on Patmos; the island
has a kind of retirement air about it, like one
of those investment homes you are always
getting invitations to come and look at. But not

really. Retirement was foreign to the apostles. And it is a hard thing for most of us to handle.

Ministers have as hard a time as anyone when it comes to retiring.

Some meet it with despondency. The minister-father of a friend of mine has been depressed since the day he moved his office out of the church. In and out of the hospital three or four times a year. Can't adjust. Still wants to be in the saddle, up in the pulpit, out on his calls.

An old Moravian minister I met in North Carolina says he often feels like Jonah: "All thy waves and thy billows have gone over me." His faith is eroded, he says; he needs people around him—the constant interchange, the piranha bowl—in order to believe. "God help me," he says, "it's awful!"

Of course, there are some who react positively to retirement. Like Hardin King, a friend of mine who plays golf every morning except Sunday and says he can't find time to do all the things he forgot to do while he was active in the ministry. Or George Buttrick, the great New York minister and chaplain to Harvard University, who when he was eighty-three years old was still spending half a day in his study working at some new book or sermon, relishing the time to sharpen his wits, although they always seemed sharp enough already.

But whether viewed positively or negatively, retirement is a time of rethinking and transition and reordering of life. One old retiree in our parish had some calling cards printed to go with his new status in life. In the center they stated his name: JO BANKS, RETIRED. Around that, in the four corners and in small print, were these four pieces of information: No Business, No Address, No Phone, No Money. Retirement is a time of adjustment, of reviewing the past and previewing the future. There are negotiations to be conducted, tradeoffs to be made, bargains to be struck. And, as at every other transition stage of life, there are both dangers and opportunities.

It is easy enough to fall into despair if one focuses only on the past and oneself. W. R. Inge, the famous Dean of St. Paul's in London, wrote in his autobiography of the depression that haunted him much of his life and became almost overbearing in his latter years. "How often, when I am awake at night," he said, "I seem to see a procession of grinning goblins, each saying, 'Look at me. I am what you did and

said and thought, and left undone.' " The
goblins are there, if we want to look at them—
opportunities missed, people neglected, the
gospel undeclared, a life undisciplined and
unshaped, and on and on.

H. H. Farmer, in one of his books, tells the
story of a minister friend who was stabbed to
the heart by the realization of how he sometimes
failed people. The minister had been out all day,
busy as only ministers think they are busy, and
had come in tired and grateful to a lonely house.

He had no sooner taken off his shoes and
loosened his collar and sat down to enjoy a drink
than there came a tap at the door. Grumbling
to himself, he padded off to the door and opened
it on a poor woman selling cottons. Her thick,
straggly hair fell upon the very worn collar of
an old overcoat, and her eyesight was apparently
very poor, for she wore extremely thick-lensed
spectacles and was led around by an ill-kempt,
underfed boy of perhaps twelve or thirteen.

"I am afraid," said the minister, "I cut short
a tale of domestic woe with a very sharp no
because I was so tired." The boy, taking the
woman by the hand, said, "Come away, mum,"
and led her out the walk to the street. As he
turned back to shut the gate, said the minister,

there was on his face the purest look of hatred one ever saw. It seemed to reveal a distillation of all the pain and suffering the boy had ever known.

The minister shut the door, went back into his study, fell on his knees, and cried, "God, be merciful to me, a sinner!"

I often think of that story at the end of a day, and I wonder how many people I have disappointed in the course of pastoral rounds because I was inattentive to some cry for help or disinterested in the tale some poor soul was hopeful of pouring out. Each time, I think, "Oh, I will be more careful tomorrow! God help me to be sensitive!" But what will it be like to have such thoughts at the end of my ministry, when there will be no tomorrow for making amends?

And as for family—oh my, how much we have to answer for on that score! I remember the pathos in the voice of one minister—he was about sixty, I think—as he described his regret at not having had more time for his wife and children. "It is the great failing of my life," he said. "I always had time for church people, at any hour of the day or night. But now my children are grown and I realize I don't even know them. They got only the dregs of my life, nothing more. One son hardly speaks to me. I don't blame him. It's unforgivable! And my wife—she doesn't say anything, but I tremble to think how many evenings she has spent alone, how many meals she has eaten without another soul at the table with her, how many times she has gone to bed in a silent house. I wish I had it all to live over!"

Which of us cannot partake of his sorrow?

Maybe part of our homework at the time of transition from late midlife into retirement is a personal prayer of confession, some word of our own expression in which we admit to God what a botch we have made of things and ask to be shriven in order to turn with healthy minds and hearts to the new business that lies ahead. Would it run something like this?

O God of the ages, in the folds of whose arms lies my only forgiveness, I confess to you my deep inadequacy for the years of serving my calling. I have been proud and stiff-necked, and have gone my own way in solving problems, dealing with other people's needs, and declaring the Word. I have spent too little time listening, either to you or to those around me, and now feel despair because I know my own failure better than I know anything else in life. Take away my sin, O God, and heal my brokenness. Repair my life that I may yet glorify your name. Through Jesus Christ my Lord. Amen.

And God, who hears every prayer of a broken and contrite heart, will forgive our sin and put his spirit within us, that we may walk in the light and not in the darkness. How many times have we said the words to others? Will God cast us away because we are worse than they?

The irony is that God loves sinners because he is able to be so much more himself among them than he is with the righteous, of whom there are so few.

I said it is easy to fall into despair if we focus on ourselves and our shortcomings. It is also easy to find joy and peace if we focus on God and what he does. We need to confess; there is no way around that. We do not get off the hook by letting ourselves off. But, having confessed and had our vision renewed, we are able to see, with new clarity from our new vantage point, how rich is the panorama of grace in all our lives!

Retirement is a great time to learn about rehearsal theology, if one has never understood it before. It is a time for retrospection, for looking back across the hills and valleys of one's own existence and noting where the Almighty God has intervened in one's path, lifting a burden here and introducing a surprise there! That's what the Hebrews did, of course. They were not sophisticated theologians, but they knew where they had met the Lord; they remembered and talked about those places. And that is what we need to do in retirement. We need to trace our journey—write our autobiography, as it were—and realize how wonderful the God of the covenant has been.

I had an experience recently—a right-brain experience—that will be part of my theology as long as I live. It took me back to my youth, when I was an inexperienced boy of sixteen trying to learn to pray beside my bed in the semi-attic room where I slept. One night, as I prayed, I saw an angel. He stood in the corner of the room, translucent yet the source of light, silent as a stone. I knew instinctively it was Gabriel; I don't know why. He was like a human being in form, yet different. His hair was silver, yet not silver but made of light. His hands were long and slender, and graceful as poetry. For years I puzzled about the meaning of that visitation. Why were there no words? Was there something wrong in my receiver, that I heard nothing? It seemed an inferior apparition, and I was to blame.

But, to return to the more recent story, I was absolutely drained of energy, limp as a rag but tense as a post. I had not had a vacation since Lent, and had added to my usual duties four or five outside speaking and travel engagements. On top of that, we were building a new house and trying to pack for a deadline move. And, still on top of that, I was attempting to plan and write these messages on Christ and the seasons of ministry. My hands had begun to shake, and I was awaking very early every morning with anxieties flitting through my mind like ghosts in a haunted house. Desperately I tried to renew my prayer life, to dig deeper, to find the resources of Spirit to cope with my failing strength and resolve.

One morning, when the waves of despair were nearly suffocating me, I lay in bed and tried to practice fantasy praying, the kind my friend Wayne Pipkin used when he received the message that Christ is born today. Where, I wondered, is a peaceful place in this wide earth? And I remembered the seacoast and the tiny village of Piso Lavadhi, on the island of Paros in the Greek Mediterranean. My oldest son and I had taken a backpacking trip through the islands when he graduated from high school, and had stayed several days in Piso Lavadhi because of its extreme beauty and quietness.

In my mind, I projected myself back in Piso Lavadhi, walking along the road by the sea, staring at the shifting shadows on the rocks at the bottom of the clear water. Then I was aware of a ship sailing into the harbor a thousand yards away, and I knew, just as Wayne Pipkin had known there was a message in the bottle for him, that someone on that ship had come there to see me, to bring me a message I needed to hear.

I ran around the harbor to be at the dock just as the gangplank was dropped. Funny, as I ran I became aware that the ship was a fifteenth- or sixteenth-century galleon, and when I arrived at the dock I saw that the sailors were all dressed in an ancient manner. I don't know why that was.

Precisely as I arrived at the lowered gangplank, the most important character on the ship was beginning his descent to meet me. He too was dressed in ancient costume, that of a warrior with ballooned armor and helmet.

Looking back, I realize that he looked very much like the famous painting by Rembrandt known as "Man with the Golden Helmet."

But it was Gabriel! It was the angel who had appeared in my garret room those thirty-two, almost thirty-three, years before! And he said, "I have been with you all the time."

That's all: "I have been with you all the time."

I tell you, my heart leapt up.

It was what I needed to hear.

He had been there the *whole* time—since I was a boy.

For days, when the waves of desperation came over me, I remembered. I will always remember.

Rehearsal theology. God has been with us *here* and *here* and *here* and *here*. That is for retirement, isn't it?

And more.

In retirement, we have more time to be with him. To practice the Presence. To experience the indwelling Spirit. To be in touch with God.

Oh, we'll do other things too. Retirement is the time to follow all the roads not taken in one's youth and early life, when options had to be narrowed in order to make a living and get one's work done. Time to laugh and play and take acting lessons and paint in oils and learn to play bridge and go scuba diving and all the rest. Montaigne said, "There is nothing more remarkable in the life of Socrates than that he found time in his old age to learn to dance and play on instruments and thought it was time well spent."

But learning to pray better—to practice the Presence—is the most important thing of all. It's—well, it's getting ready.

One of our favorite people is an elderly nun named Sister Anastasia—Sister "Resurrection." Sister was a wonderful piano teacher during a long and happy career. But when Sister became too old to teach any longer, her mother superior called her in one day and said, "Sister, it is time for you to move on to other things. From now on, you will spend your days in prayer." And Sister began a new phase of her career, going into the chapel each day to pray for all the people on her list, and hold them up before God.

I am glad to say we are on Sister's list. And if there is anything particularly happy or successful about our family, it is at least partially owing to Sister Anastasia's prayers for us. Hers is a wonderful way to spend one's latter years. And it is something we can all do. We can retire into God, so to speak.

I said retirement is "getting ready." It is. Gradually, surely, the flesh is purged away and everything becomes Spirit. All those things that Paul said are works of the flesh—fornication, idolatry, sorcery, unrest, and so on—fade away from our interest. And all the things that are fruits of the Spirit—joy, peace, love, gentleness, kindness, self-control—simply fill our lives to overflowing.

And our way of looking at things sort of completes its metamorphosis, a metamorphosis begun years before when we first became aware of the indwelling Christ. Everything seems different. We know what Paul meant when he talked about "keeping the faith" and about being "found" in Christ, not having his own righteousness, which is of the law, but the righteousness that comes through the faith of Christ.

Paul didn't say "the faith *in* Christ," but "the faith *of* Christ." That is, the faithfulness of Christ, the obedience of Christ, the discipline of Christ, that kept both him and Paul to the end. We have that, too—faithfulness, obedience, discipline. That's what produces the fruits of the Spirit and the joy of these latter years.

I read a beautiful little story somewhere about a boy and an old man sitting on a dock in the late afternoon, fishing. They talked about many things—why sunsets are red, why the rain falls, why the seasons change, what life is like. Finally the boy looked up at the old man, as the old man was baiting his hook for him, and asked, "Does anybody ever see God?" "Son," said the old man, looking across the blue waters, "it's getting so I hardly see anything else."

That's it, isn't it?

That's the way retirement ought to be.

That's the way ministry ought to wind down.

"Son, it's getting so I hardly see anything else."

And then the words will come: "Welcome, beloved servant. You have been faithful over a few things; behold, I will make you ruler over many."

# Prayer

Life in all its hues
is beautiful, Lord, like the rainbow.
Forgive us if we have been
too busy to notice.
Help us to make time for you.
Teach us to see you everywhere.
And give us the eternal rest
that is promised to your servants.
Through Jesus Christ our Lord,
AMEN.